WOOD PALLET WORKSHOP

WOOD PALLET WORKSHOP

20 DIY Projects that Turn Forgotten Wood into Stylish Home Furnishings

DANNY DARKE

Skyhorse Publishing

Skyhorse Publishing books may be purchased in bulk at special discounts for sales promotion, corporate gifts, fund-raising, or educational purposes. Special editions can also be created to specifications. For details, contact the Special Sales Department, Skyhorse Publishing, 307 West 36th Street, 11th Floor, New York, NY 10018 or info@skyhorsepublishing.com.

Visit our website at www.skyhorsepublishing.com.

10 9 8 7 6 5 4 3

Library of Congress Cataloging-in-Publication Data is available on file.

Cover design by Jane Sheppard
Cover photo credit: Danny Darke

Print ISBN: 978-1-5107-0527-2
Ebook ISBN: 978-1-5107-0528-9

Printed in China

Dedication

To my parents, who gave me a sense of humor; my sisters, who are so jealous right now; my extended family (I can't name everyone, just Joey); Hannah, whose mistakes I learned from; Monica, for letting me write a book; and finally to Chris and Frankie, who mean so much to me that I cannot express it here.

CONTENTS

Introduction

Part of the charm in working with pallets is that they are imperfect. After being used and reused, all boards are not necessarily created equal, thereby giving you, the designer, freedom to create outside the bounds of perfection. Pallet projects usually have a personalized, non-conforming look to them, in a word: unique. Wood pallets give people of any skill level the opportunity to transform unused and unwanted materials into something of value, artistic or practical. Reinventing an old pallet is a great way to recycle unwanted material that would otherwise be thrown away or go to waste, so you're helping the environment while also being savvy by not spending too much (or any) money. I have been creating projects from pallets for years, and when people walk into my home and ask, "Where did *that* come from?" they're shocked to find out that I made it!

Before you get started, there are a couple of things you should know that will make your life easier. In this book, you will learn simple ways to use pallets to create a variety of items, from basic shelves and serving trays to larger furniture, such as an industrial-style coffee table and a rustic headboard. With upcycling old furniture, one would usually have to scavenge weekly garbage routes hoping to find the right item or pay for it at a yard sale or online, but pallets are free, consistently available, and come in different shapes and sizes, allowing anyone to pick one out and imagine it as something else, regardless of skill level. I always try to create in the simplest, least expensive way possible while still making quality pieces that will last. All of the projects shown can be made with common tools that you likely have or can easily access.

PALLET BACKGROUND

Variations of Pallets

Pallets come in a variety of forms. Since I mostly gather pallets wherever I can get them, I never know which ones I'll find. The first thing I look for in a pallet is one that isn't warped and has lots of deck boards or slats. The more boards that match from a single pallet, the better they are for making furniture. The two most common types that I come across are stringer and block pallets.

Stringer Pallets

A stringer design is a pallet that has "stringers," or long pieces of wood, that run the length of the pallet and sit in between the top deck boards and the bottom deck boards. Stringers are often preferable over block pallets because they are lighter and easier to dismantle. Cutting a deck board off a block is not my favorite part of my day. That being said, they definitely have their place: block pallets are generally stronger and the boards are less likely to be damaged.

Block Pallets

A block design is a pallet that has a thick rectangular or square "block" that creates space between the top and bottom deck boards. There are usually four blocks, one in each corner as well as one spaced between each corner for a total of eight. I say "usually" because I have seen all kinds of shapes and sizes in pallets. This is because there are also recycled pallets that have been either repaired for further use or manufactured out of recycled materials so you never know what kind of monstrosities you could find with one of those.

Wing Pallets

Another type of pallet you may come across fairly often is a wing pallet. They are similar to a stringer with the most noticeable difference being that the deck boards extend longer past the stringer board giving it a "winged" look. They are delightful and I use them all the time.

Boarded Pallets

The close-boarded pallet can have stringer boards or blocks between deck boards. They can be extremely heavy but make the best coffee tables, benches, and desks because they are smooth, sturdy, and usually even, giving you a leg up when building a piece of furniture that you need to be flush.

Other pallets that make appearances are plywood pallets, skids, hybrids, and a form of stringer pallets. These stringer pallets have boards placed right next to each other with no space between, and I will refer to them as close-boarded pallets. Plywood pallets have—you guessed it—a piece of plywood in place of deck boards either on one or both sides. I find these pallets to be weird and they are usually terribly warped or moldy by the time they get to me, so I rarely grab them. A skid is a mix between a close-boarded pallet and a wing pallet but with no bottom deck boards. This is the type my business is named after yet I rarely come across them.

Hybrids are pallets that subscribe to no particular form or shape and are created out of necessity or possibly by missing pieces into odd shapes or wood combinations. The term hybrid is used in a range of ways in connection to pallets, but I am using it to describe a pallet that does not easily fit into previously mentioned categories. These pallets are extremely useful although unreliable to find as you never know what to expect. Many times I have designed an item around a hybrid pallet that I found and inspired me to think in a new direction. As an example, the pallet I found for the coffee table is similar to a block or close-boarded pallet, but it only has four blocks and no bottom deck boards, so I would call it a hybrid. When I saw it, I instantly pictured a stout table. Another gem I found was the top of the pallet bar included in this book. It could have previously looked much different but as it was found, was perfect for my project. It may be a good idea to look for pallets first from time to time before settling on a design because you never know what you might find.

Hopefully this information will help steer you in the right direction when picking which pallets to take home. On a bad day, I find myself dismantling four different pallets just to get enough good pieces to build one shelf. It is so much easier to pick the right pallets to begin with!

Treated Pallets vs. Untreated Pallets

Realistically, there is no sure way to be certain that the pallet you are working with is "safe" outside of going directly to the manufacturer and getting one fresh out of the oven. Any one who is picking up used pallets will not know exactly where and what such a pallet has been exposed to. Even if the person who provides you their leftover materials tells you where they come from and what they are used for—you are still just taking their word for it. However do not let this news discourage you. You are not leading a dangerous life now because you have decided to craft with recycled materials. As with most things in life, a little common sense can guide you to safely selecting pallets.

Treated Pallets

Pallets that are marked or stamped with information tell you that it is used for export and has been treated according to the standards required by the country it was being shipped to. There are basically three different abbreviations you may come across on these stamps that will give you an indication of how a pallet—at some point in its past—was treated.

HT = Heat Treated
KD = Kiln Dried
MB = Methyl – Bromide

(A fourth abbreviation people ask about is DB which stands for "debarked," but has nothing to do with the way it is treated in connection to your health.)

A quick glance at the above treatments without any further explanation is probably enough for it to become obvious which one you should pass on. Methyl-bromide treated pallets are not commonly found anymore but may show up in older stacks of wood. To give you perspective, this pesticide is also largely used as a soil fumigant in tomato, strawberry, grape, pepper, and other popular crops. You are possibly getting some methyl-bromide whether you choose to or not, so why not avoid adding more to your daily dose by passing on using MB-stamped pallets.

Untreated Pallets

An unmarked pallet may indicate that it was not treated because it is meant for domestic use, and therefore never had to meet the standards of any other countries. Although these could be considered a safer bet, you still do not know which hazardous items they may have been used to transport.

The bottom line is as long as you try to select pallets that do not have dark, greasy spills of an unknown substance on them, do not smell strongly of chemicals, are not covered in mold or marked MB—you should be on the safe side. You will not be burning these pallets, releasing their chemicals into the air to inhale, and if you're like me, you are going to slather them in polyurethane anyway, thereby trapping any hidden toxins within.

Where to Find Pallets

I have been building with pallets for a long time, and I have never once paid for them. You shouldn't either! When I first started crafting with wood pallets, I would drive around in search of them near dumpsters. I would also peruse the Internet for listings of free pallets that I could pick up locally. I never had to go that route because I could almost always find enough by driving within five miles of my home, but it is a viable option if you are wondering where to find them.

One of the best ways to get them is to find a company that has a continuous supply of pallets that they are looking to get rid of. I have found that most of these people are happy to help. A couple years ago I pulled into a local heating and cooling company who had "the mother-load" out back. I walked inside and asked if they would mind if I took a few. They shrugged and said, "Sure, take as many as you want whenever you want. Take 'em all!" And I have been ever since!

When you're in the market for wood pallets, make sure people know about it! Once people around me knew I used pallets, they started dropping them off or telling me where they spotted a bunch of them. It's always good to have more than one option for getting your hands on some!

Pallet Safety

If you are working out of your home or garage, you will have to improvise as your space likely does not meet O.S.H.A. safety standards. Here are some tips to consider:

- Wear safety glasses when sanding or making cuts.
- Be careful when lifting pallets by yourself and try not to lift them higher than chest level, for instance when you are loading or unloading pallets from your car or truck.
- Be conscious of where all power tool cords are so as not to trip over them or have a cord get caught up short, causing your reciprocating saw to go flying out of your hands.
- Work in an area that has good ventilation.
- Pick up after yourself! You may forget about that rusty nail you removed that is now in your foot.
- If you are using a corded drill, be mindful of how powerful they are, as well as how scorching hot the screws can become when removing them with your drill.
- Do not work in bare feet or flip-flops; wear real shoes.
- If you are trying to screw into a board and the screw is making no progress, take the time to stop and drill a hole first instead of pushing as hard as you can.
- The closest calls will probably be when disassembling pallets with your reciprocating saw. Just make sure the wood you are cutting into is secured. If the entire pallet is shaking and vibrating loudly and you are having a hard time holding onto your saw, this is not a good sign and something bad is about to happen.
- Do not stick your saw somewhere low on the pallet and start cutting up towards your face, and the same goes for cutting down towards your feet. Get your body out of the direction where the blade is headed when you are applying pressure to move the saw through the wood; once free, it might pop out and get you.

By keeping these suggestions in mind and making sure you are familiar with all of your tools before using them, you will probably be all right!

Pallet Basics

Working with pallets is fairly straightforward, but there are a few things that are good to know to save yourself time.

Disassembling wood pallets is fastest, cleanest, and easiest on your body when tackled using a reciprocating saw. Be sure to fit it with a bi-metal blade that will work for metal and wood. The saw will cut right through your nail-embedded pallets. The downside to sawing off nails is that it will leave a small amount of the nail remaining in the board with a sharp edge that will need to be hammered down before sanding or it will tear your sandpaper to shreds. If you decide to disassemble with a hammer and crow bar, get ready to sweat and be careful not to force the board off before you have loosened it enough to remove with ease. This can cause your board to break, rendering it useless and putting you back at square one. Heat-treated (HT) pallets split more easily, so be especially careful if you are using a crowbar on those.

Pallet-Making Tools and Equipment

Miter saw
Reciprocating saw
Hammer
Sander
Tape measure
Pencil
Disposable paintbrushes
Polyurethane
Multipurpose screws
Corded electric drill
Wood glue
Countersink drill bit

I highly recommend using multipurpose screws over another type, such as wood screws. They are tougher and grab the wood better. I also cannot say enough about my countersink drill bit. It drills a cone-shaped hole into your board allowing the screw to sit below the surface of your board, giving you a flush finish. Disposable paintbrushes are inexpensive chip brushes that you can find at hardware or department stores for around a dollar. They are the way to go since a lot of the time you will be painting with stain, which is a waste of energy trying to wash out of any brush. Better to throw them out and be done with the fumes. Finally, I would suggest buying a corded drill over any cordless battery-operated type. I used the latter for a while, but they are not powerful enough, have to be constantly charging, and the batteries can go bad. Then you can find yourself wondering if you grabbed the good battery or the bad one and it just isn't worth the hassle. The cord is not a huge imposition and this type of drill is much more powerful.

PALLET PROJECTS

PART ONE

FURNITURE

Hanging Shelf

These shelves are probably the easiest item to make from pallets, as they are nearly formed already when you get the pallet! They can be used in a variety of ways, such as bookshelves or picture displays.

Materials used:

6 - #6 x 1¼″ multipurpose screws
$^{3}/_{32}$″ drill bit
Reciprocating or jigsaw
Sander with 60 grit paper
Stain
Electric drill

Instructions:

- When possible, use a pallet that you can get two shelves out of.

▸ Mark out your desired height and cut the pallet with a reciprocating saw.

▸ Cut off two extra boards for the bottoms of the shelves.

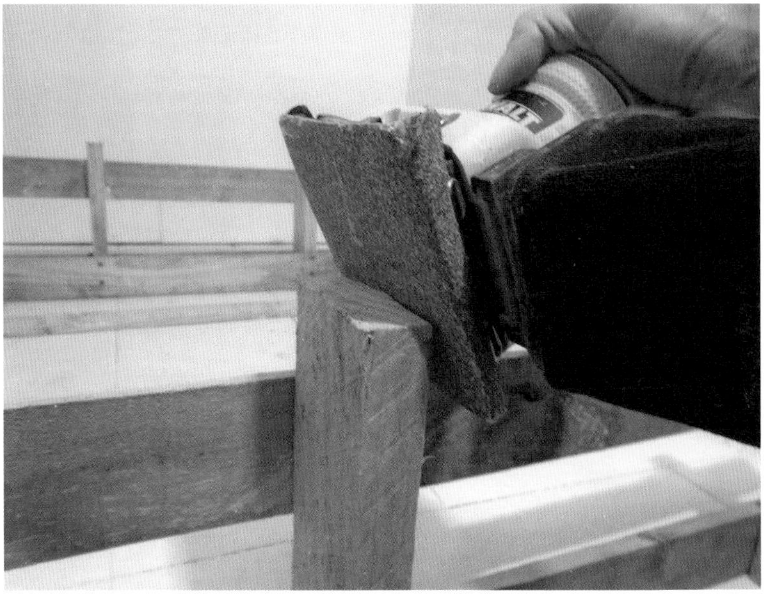

▸ Sand off the rough edges.

▸ Flip the shelf upside down to place the bottom board. Pre-drill the holes to avoid splitting the pallet wood with the screws.

Adhere the bottom piece with three multipurpose screws per shelf.

I stained mine and then sanded them again to give a weathered look.

End Table

This small table may look frail, but is quite sturdy once screwed all together. There are a lot of end tables out there for purchase, but this style is hard to find and makes it a great little addition to any room.

Materials used:

12 - #6 x 1¼″ multipurpose screws
$^{3}/_{32}$″ drill bit
Reciprocating or jigsaw
Miter saw
Sander with 60 grit paper
Acrylic paint
Stain
Polyurethane
Wood glue
Electric drill
Small nails

Instructions:

- Choose a large pallet, as you will be using most of it for the table. The table will look nicer if it is made from all the same wood.

Cut out the tabletop with a reciprocating saw.

Cut off the extra edges on bottom. This way you can have a spot under the top piece to slide in the legs and screw them into sides of open drawers.

- From the remaining pallet, measure out pieces for the legs. I cut off the entire bottom section three boards high because it measured out perfectly for making two equal leg pieces.

- Cut the wood in half.

- You will only need one side of a pallet for the legs. Remove the other side with a saw.

- Remove the top horizontal stringer support. Use the bottom horizontal stringer support as a place to rest the shelf.

- Set up your table in a general way to measure the size of the shelf.

- Use the remaining pallet wood to cut out the shelf boards.

▸ Sand all of the pieces and assemble the boards for the shelf. I like to use thin support slats and glue them on the underside of shelf boards so they don't show too much.

▸ After the glue dries, hammer in a couple of nails for extra support.

- Rest the tabletop on another object so you can line up the leg piece to screw it into the side.

- Use one multipurpose screw for the top of each leg board (three per side). Turn the table around and screw in the remaining leg piece on opposite side.

▸ Pre-drill the holes into the lip of shelf to avoid splitting the boards with the screws.

▸ Set the shelf onto the lip and screw in the shelf piece. Use three screws at each end of the shelf for a total of six on the entire shelf.

- Paint the table with acrylic paint (in this case, bright red).

- Finish the wood with a dark polyshade, which has stain and polyurethane. Wipe the surface with a clean cloth after applying so that the red still shows up.

This nice, bright piece makes the room a little more interesting!

Bench

Although a pallet bench might not be the first choice in your room for seating, it is perfect for sitting a moment to take shoes off by the door, or for extra seating when hosting a large group of people. It is also lightweight and nice to have when you need to move around to accommodate guests in different parts of your home. If you would like to make it cozier, just throw a couple cushions on top and you are set!

Materials used:

24 - #6 x 1¼″ multipurpose screws
4 - #6 x 2″ multipurpose screws
Reciprocating or jigsaw
Miter saw
Sander with 60 grit paper
Electric drill
Acrylic paint
Stain
Polyurethane

Instructions:

- Find the perfect pallet. If you are able to find a nice pallet like this close-boarded stringer, you will already have your bench top constructed and just need to sand and make a couple cuts to finish it off!

- Using a reciprocating or jigsaw, cut the pallet in half, making sure you cut on the outside of the middle stringer board, leaving you with the top of your bench already nailed together on each side.

- Turn the bench to the underside and remove the top and bottom deck boards to make room for the bench legs.

- It is important to reattach underside boards because this is what keeps your bench stable. Screw them into new spots, closer to center with four 1¼″ screws apiece.

- Find solid stringer boards to cut four legs and two support boards.

- Line up the bench legs to the underside corners and drill holes for the screws, starting with two on the side of the bench to screw in horizontally.

- Drill two screws through the top of the bench down vertically, as well. You will need a total of four screws per leg for a total of eight 1¼″ screws.

- Cut two support boards that measure the width of the bench legs at each end.

- Screw supports into legs with 2″ screws, one at each end of support for a total of four screws.

This bench seems to be made for this spot. I painted it with white and then added definition to the edges of each board with dark stain. Finished with polyurethane.

Bar

A pallet bar can be used inside the home or outdoors. You can make them vertical for high stools or standing, or build them horizontally to be more table-like. Once assembled, they are very heavy and strenuous to move. If possible, I suggest assembling the piece where you will be using it. This tall bar is great for outside, when you want to take a break from gardening, or when barbecuing with friends.

Materials used:

6 large steel mending braces
52 - #6 x 1¼″ multipurpose screws
20 - #6 x 2″ screws
Wood glue
Reciprocating saw
Miter saw
Stain
Polyurethane

Instructions:

- First, find two block pallets that match.

- Use flat, smooth, solid pieces for the top of the bar as it will have to stand up to people leaning or resting their arms on it.

- This is the frame for the top of the bar. It may be a hybrid pallet, but it can easily be crafted with four long stringer boards and two short boards for ends regardless. Use twenty 2″ screws to assemble. Screw in six on each long stringer duo to secure, and four on each short board to screw down into long pieces.

- Use the reciprocating saw to get the deck boards for your bar top. Sand smooth.

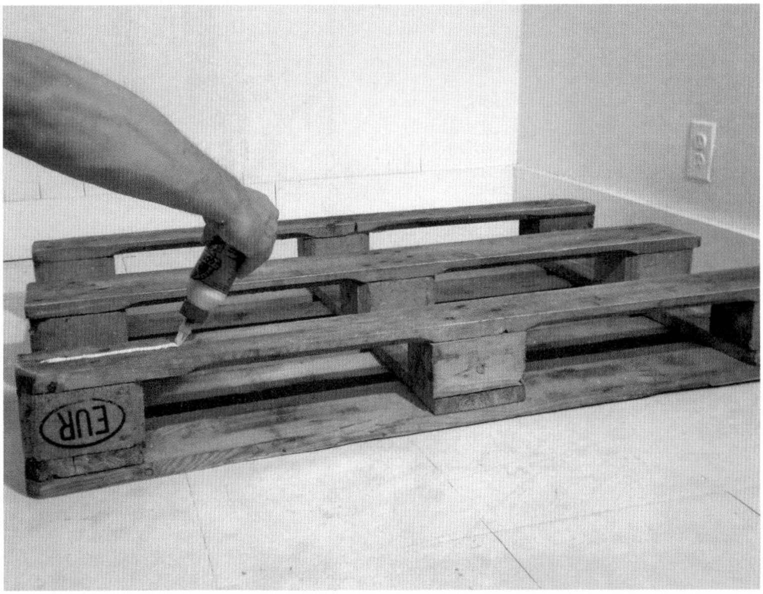

- Now it is time to assemble the bar base. Lay one of your block pallets with the bottom deck boards facing up. Apply the wood glue.

- You can use a generous amount, but keep in mind that the glue is just to help keep the pallets from moving when screwing in mending braces. The glue will not be strong enough to lift the base horizontally and keep it together.

- Now take the second pallet and carefully place it on top, making sure the blocks are lined up so you can screw the braces in straight. Allow the glue to dry for thirty minutes.

▸ Screw in the mending braces. The braces shown used six 1¼″ screws each.

▸ The deck boards will need supports to screw into, so cut two pieces to fit into frame at each end. Make sure you leave enough space between the supports to allow the bar top to fit over the bar base with block pallets sitting inside long stringer sides. You can glue these to the inside of the frame or just hammer them into place, as they will be secure once you screw deck boards into them.

- Screw deck boards into vertical support boards and horizontal side stringers with ten 1¼″ screws, two per board.

- It is a good idea to use a countersink bit while pre-drilling the holes for the screws, so no screw heads will be sticking above the bar's surface.

- Now, stand the bar base up and set the top of bar in place. Screw the bar top into the block of base if possible for tightest bond. Use six 1¼″ screws (three per pallet), one for each block.

- This bar was so heavy and awkward in my house, but I love it outside! For a style like this one, use a green stain, or another color of your choice, and finish with polyurethane. Paint the mending braces to give it a more finished look.

Chest

Here is a sturdy piece of furniture that is timeless. With this project, it is very important to get all of the pieces aligned evenly so the top closes tightly. This chest usually takes the longest to make because of the small adjustments needed here and there, depending how straight or thick the deck boards you are using come out. With a little (or a lot of) patience, you can build this chest to any size you like and customize with a range of hinges and latches to accompany the look you are going for. I use this handsome piece for video game storage next to the TV, but it can also be used to hold small blankets next to the couch for cold nights, or even as a coffee table!

Materials used:

36 - #6 x 1¼″ multipurpose screws
24 - #6 x ⅝″ screws
6 L-brackets
2 - ½″ metal hinges
1 metal latch
Reciprocating saw
Miter saw
Electric drill
Sander with 60 grit paper
Stain

Instructions:

- This project takes a lot of wood. Try to find the straightest boards you can, it will make this go so much easier.

- These boards will be used for the sides and trim. I chose boards that differ slightly in color to add contrast.

Make your cuts for the front and back panels. Use all the same boards by cutting them in half if possible so that the chest looks uniform. Sand the boards.

Make the cuts for the side panels. Sand the boards.

- Cut four pieces of trim for the side panels, sand, and screw them on using 1¼″ screws.

- Glue two braces on the insides of the panels to hold them together. The reason behind this is you are going to want to line up the front and back panels to the sides before you get an exact measurement for how long to cut the trim for the front/back pieces as the trim will extend out, covering the side pieces.

- Pre-drill the holes for the screws to make sure all of the screws go in nice and easy. Screw the side panels into the front and back panels.

- Now that you have all four sides lined up, measure how long you will need to cut trim pieces. Sometimes at this point, the boards may have moved slightly. To avoid this, I recommend measuring step-by-step as the project progresses.

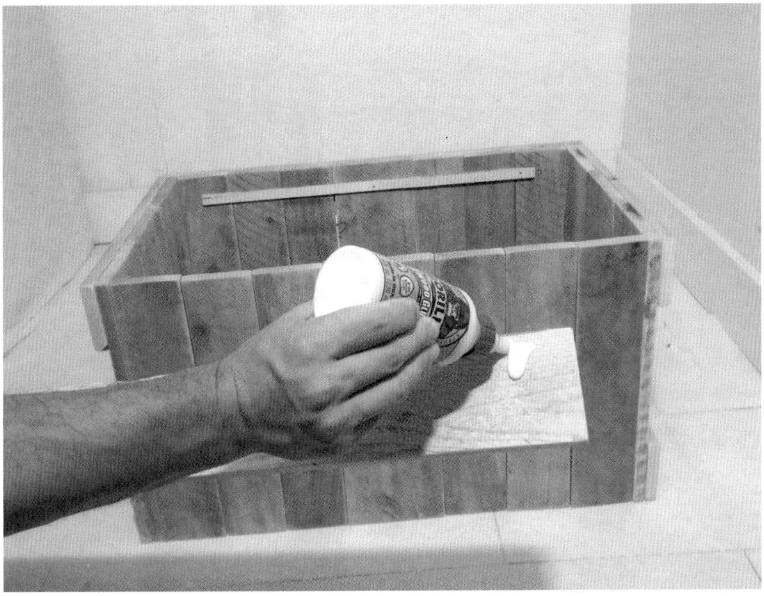

▸ After making the cuts and sanding, glue your four pieces of trim on the front and back panels for extra support.

▸ Drill the holes for the screws to attach the trim pieces into the side panel trim pieces.

- Clamp and allow the pieces to dry for thirty minutes. Then screw in the front and back trim to the side trim.

- Make the cut for the bottom pieces, sand, and fit them inside to see if you need to make any adjustments on size.

▸ Fit inside and attach to lower side planks using L-brackets and $\frac{5}{8}''$ screws.

▸ Use two L-brackets per bottom board for a total of six.

- Make cuts for the top piece, sand, and again fit on top to ensure that they cover the entire rim around the chest top.

- Cut two boards to keep top pieces together. Position them on the inside of the top boards in a way that they will just fit inside the chest when closed, so as to grab the sides and secure the chest shut.

Measure placements for the hinges on the back. There is more than one way to use the hinges; the one shown is the easiest method I have found.

Screw in the hinges. Most hinges will come with their own set of screws.

- Measure the exact middle location for your latch.

- Screw the latch into place.

- It will have to line up with corresponding piece on the top plank. Like the hinges, the latches will come with screws in most cases.

- You are done! Move the top up and down to see if you need to tighten up the hinges and ensure that the latch is correctly placed.

- I like the wood to stand out on the chests, so I used a light-colored stain to bring out the darker parts of the wood and protect it from liquids or stains. This chest would look good anywhere!

Headboard

Making your own headboard is a great way to save money and get exactly what you want. Bedroom sets can be rather expensive, especially if you are looking for something unique. This project is straightforward to do but can be cumbersome, so I would suggest either assembling it close to the room you will be using it in or planning on possibly breaking it down before moving it when it's complete. You can add hooks, lights, or use it for shelving to add functionality to your piece.

Materials used:

32 - #6 x 1¼″ multipurpose screws
4 - #6 x 2″ multipurpose screws
Reciprocating or jigsaw
Miter saw
Sander with 60 grit paper
Stain

Instructions:

- Find a large pallet to use as the framework. If you are making this for a queen-sized bed or larger, you will want long stringers. Many industrial companies will have extra pallets of this size.

▸ For a queen-sized mattress, you will need multiple deck boards of at least 40″ in length to assure you do not see where the boards end. It is not as necessary with this project to find boards that are exactly the same width, color, or look, so pick out whichever boards you like and sand them smooth.

▸ You will need three stringers for the frame, two long deck boards for cross braces to screw the headboard planks into, and one more for the top trim.

- Cut the stringer boards to your desired length with the miter saw. Screw three stringers together attaching horizontal stringer to vertical sides with two 2″ screws at the top of each sideboard for a total of four screws.

- Since the side frame stringers are only attached at the top, there will be a lot of movement, so make sure to cut your cross brace boards the same length as the top of your frame as it is now. When screwing both braces (especially the lowest cross brace), move the side stringers to your liking so that they hit your cross boards evenly. Screw in each brace board with four 1¼″ screws, two on each end. You could also add one in the middle of the top cross brace to secure it to the frame.

- Cut the top trim board, leaving extra length over each side to add embellishments. Sand the piece, and then screw in the trim with three 1¼″ screws.

- Arrange the headboard planks to your liking and screw each board into each cross brace with one screw in each spot. You will have a total of two 1¼″ screws per plank.

- Stand the headboard up to see if there are any unruly boards that need extra attention and to make sure the frame is solid.

- I used three different shades of stain on the selected boards. I let it dry for a couple of days to make sure it was free of fumes before bringing it inside.

Deck Chair

It is not easy to find perfect pallets for deck chairs! Plan on reassembling most pallets an inch here and there so that they fit together just right. I ended up locating two that would work, but it took some driving around. This chair is a lounge-style and low to the ground. It's great for relaxing by the pool or around a fire pit.

Materials used:

12 - #6 x 1¼″ multipurpose screws
10 - #6 x 2″ multipurpose screws
Reciprocating saw
Miter saw
Sander with 60 grit paper
Electric drill
Acrylic paint
Stain
Polyurethane

Instructions:

- Find similar sized pallets and extra boards for legs, supports, and trim. Your outside stringer boards on the backrest pallet will have to be slightly wider than those of the pallet you are using as the seat (or vise-versa) so that you can fit them in next to each other.

- Remove boards on each pallet at the location where you will be joining them.

- Set the seat piece on the floor and measure the width of the middle stringer board.

- Remove enough of the middle stringer on the backrest pallet to allow room for two pallets to fit together.

- Slide the pallets together to see if you have the right fit or need to make further adjustments to either piece.

- Screw the backrest pallet into the seat pallet with four 2″ screws, two on each side.

- Cut two support pieces for the back of the chair.

- Screw supports in at the top behind the backrest pallet, joining them to the seat pallet at the bottom with 1¼″ screws. Use four per support board for a total of eight.

- Using a reciprocating or jigsaw, cut off the end of the last bottom deck board piece on each side of the seat pallet to make room for the legs.

- Lean the chair at the desired angle and then measure the outside height from the seat edge to the ground.

- Also measure the inside height from the seat to the ground. Mark the leg board with both measurements, drawing a straight line between them. Make your cut with the miter saw and the outcome will be a leg piece with an angled cut at the top. Screw in the leg pieces with three 2″ screws per piece for a total of six screws.

- Measure the bottom front of the chair to get the length of the final trim piece, which will also add support.

- Screw the trim into place with four 1¼″ screws, two on each end.

- Sand the chair to your liking. I left mine a little rough-looking everywhere except the area used for seating. I painted it mango, brushed dark stain over it, and wiped some off. Finished with polyurethane.

Coffee Table

Coffee tables are one of the most used pieces of furniture in the home. You want to create one that is stylish and will last for a long time. These tables can be as easy or detailed as you have time and effort for. I made a very simple table and added metal embellishments that are functional in style but also add an industrial flair.

Materials used:

8 steel mending braces
48 - #6 x $\frac{5}{8}''$ screws
Wood glue
Reciprocating or jigsaw
Miter saw
Sander with 60 grit paper
Acrylic paint
Stain
Polyurethane

Instructions:

- Find the perfect pallet. If you cannot find a close-boarded pallet you like to start with, you could also assemble the tabletop board-by-board with hand-picked deck boards. Attach them to stringer boards or blocks underneath to achieve a similar look to this.

- Find equal blocks that you can disassemble from another pallet and that will sit flush with each other. Remove the blocks with reciprocating saw and sand.

- Set up blocks in a desired position. When screwing in the mending braces, apply a generous amount of wood glue to help keep the tabletop in place.

- After sanding the tabletop, set it on top of the blocks and make small adjustments. Your primary concern should be that the outer sides of the blocks line up evenly with the outer sides of the tabletop so you can evenly attach braces. Allow the glue to dry for thirty minutes.

- Drill the holes for ⅝″ screws; sometimes the blocks can be very tough to screw into, so this makes it easier. Finally, screw in the mending braces in locations on each block that offer the best bond with the top to bottom. These braces require six screws per brace for a total of forty-eight screws.

- I left the mending braces as-is because I like the combination of wood and metal. This table is very low and works well as a footrest, too! This table is painted a shade of aqua. I then rubbed dark stain over it using a rag, and finished it with polyurethane.

PART TWO

HOME

Wall-Hanging Mason Jar Organizer

These jars come in handy for toiletries, kitchen items, treats for pets, and look especially lovely as flower vases! The clamps can seem tricky to attach, but once you get them on, these jars can handle a lot of wear and tear. Mason jars are cheap and can be found at most department, grocery, and hardware stores. I have found them at thrift stores for as little as ten cents!

Materials used:

3 mason jars
3 hose clamps
3 - #6 x ¾″ multipurpose screws
Reciprocating or jigsaw
Miter saw
Sander with 60 grit paper
Phillips head screwdriver

Instructions:

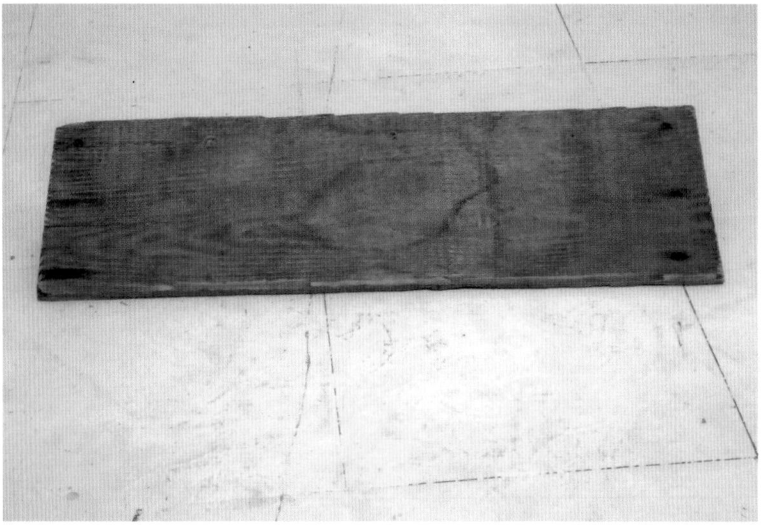

- Use a board that is on the thicker side, at least ¾″ thick. This sturdy backing is necessary for screwing in the hose clamps.

- Choose the spacing for your clamps and pre-drill the holes for the screws.

- This part can be a pain! I highly recommend using multipurpose screws. They go in the easiest, though you will need to put some effort into screwing the clamps on securely.

- Screw in all three.

- Hold jar at desired drop and tighten clamps with a Phillips head screwdriver.

- The jars I chose were already shiny, so I left this piece natural with no finish to give it a rustic look. Hang the piece by screwing it directly into the wall because the jars are glass and will be handled frequently. If you anticipate filling the jars with heavy contents, I recommend screwing it into a stud in the wall.

— Pallet-Mounted — Bottle Opener

This is a big hit with the guys! The pallet-mounted bottle opener is definitely one item that gets used more than any of the others I have made. There are so many different styles of wall-mountable bottle openers on the Internet, from different beer brewers to favorite sports teams, and all are relatively cheap. When mounting the piece, make sure that the wood is attached to the wall securely because of the pressure applied when used.

Materials used:

Wall-mountable bottle opener
Miter saw
Sander with 60 grit paper
Wood glue
2 - #6 x ⅝″ screws
Acrylic paint
Polyurethane

Instructions:

- Use straight, even deck boards for your bottle opener. It will be held together by wood glue, so you will need the edges to meet together well.

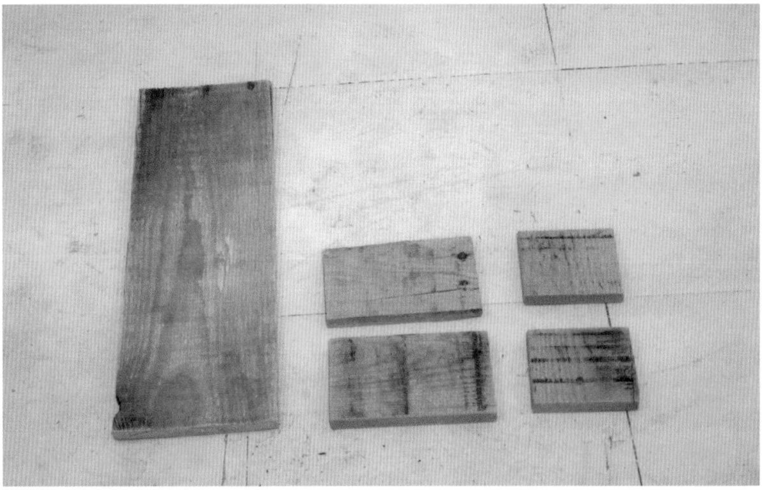

- Cut a piece as your backboard, making two cuts (the same width as the back board) for the bottom and the front of your cap catcher box. The two side cuts should be shorter. They should not be as wide as the front and bottom pieces because they will fit in between the back, front, and bottom boards.

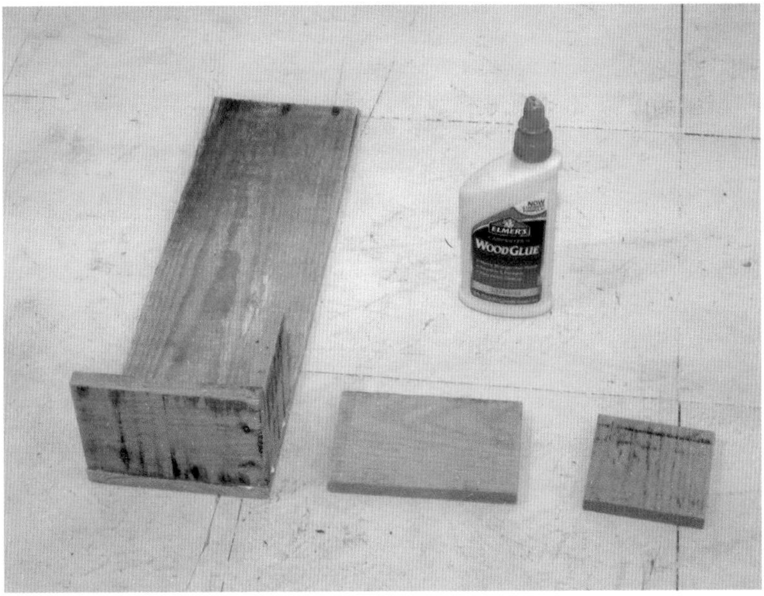

▸ Glue on the bottom and right side piece first so they can lean against each other.

▸ Glue in the left side. Apply a layer of glue around the exposed rim where you will set the front piece.

Place the final piece.

Gently wipe off any excess glue.

- Screw in the bottle opener with two $\frac{5}{8}''$ screws at the desired height.

- Paint the bottle opener with acrylic paint and cover with polyurethane to protect it from any spills. To make sure your bottle opener stands up to the pressure of repeated use, it is a good idea to try and find a stud to screw directly into instead of just hanging it on the wall. Screw the bottle opener into a secure section of wall to prevent damage from repeated use.

Towel Rack

If you think this just looks like a pallet shelf flipped upside down, you're right! In addition to functioning as a towel rack, this can also be used to hang toilet paper in the bathroom, or a paper towel holder or spice rack in the kitchen.

Materials used:

$\frac{3}{32}$″ drill bit
¾″ spade drill bit
3 - #6 x 1¼″ multipurpose screws
Reciprocating or jigsaw
Sander with 60 grit paper
Tension rod
Stain
Electric drill

Instructions:

- The length of the cut piece should account for the ¾″ holes you will drill on each stringer board end.

- Cut off an extra board for the top of the towel rack.

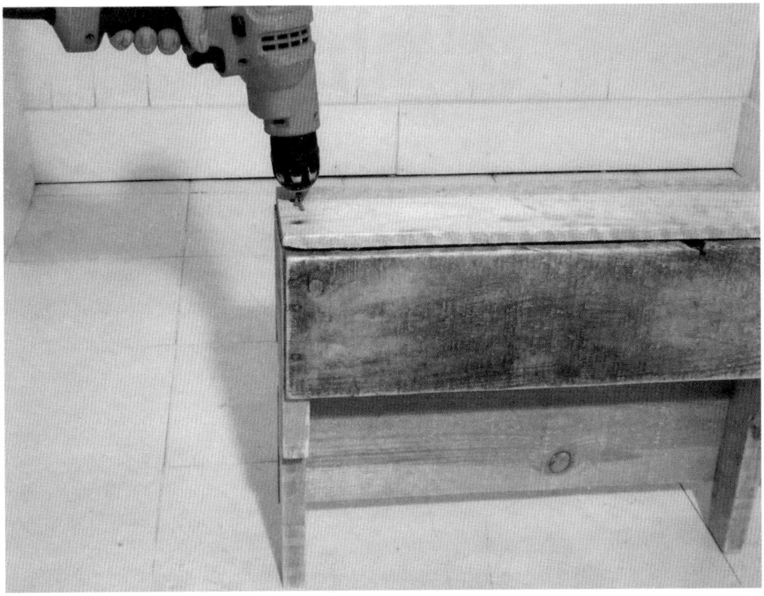

- Sand the pieces, fit the extra board on top of the towel rack, and pre-drill holes for screws to prevent the pallet board from splitting.

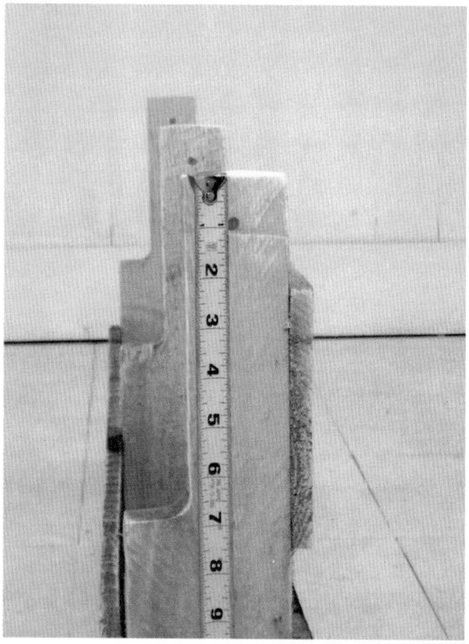

▸ Screw in three multipurpose screws with an electric drill into the stringer board supports.

▸ Measure and mark exactly where you want to drill holes for the tension rod.

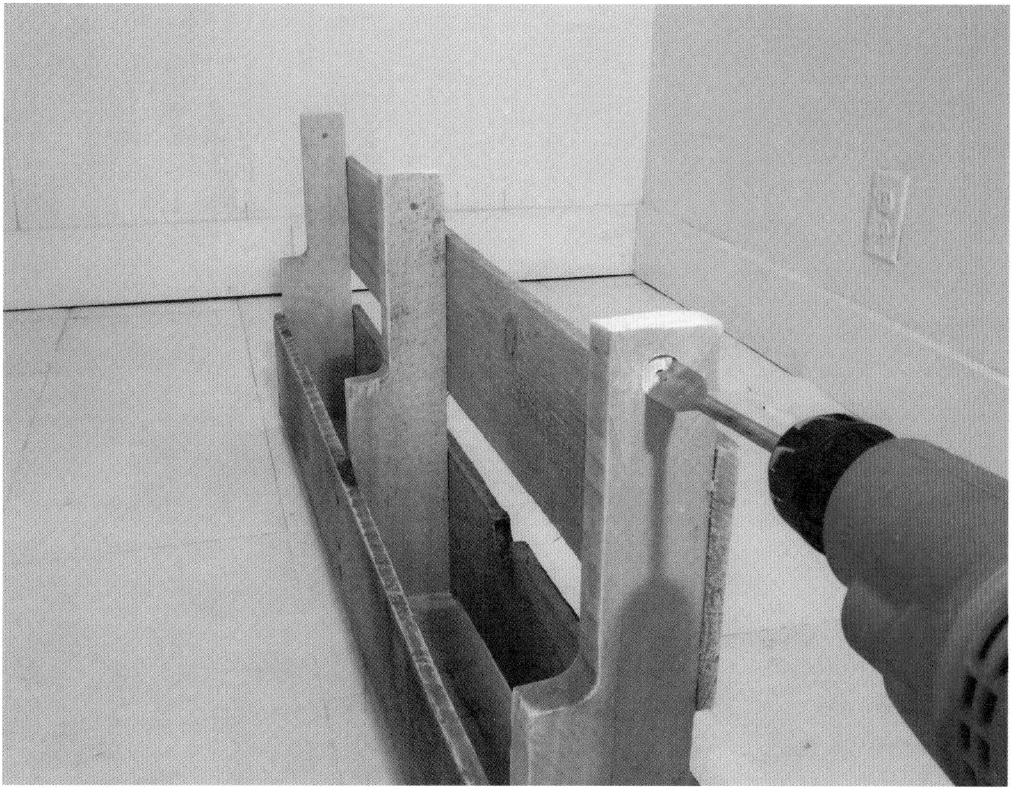

- Use a spade drill bit to drill the holes. These drill bits require more strength than regular bits, so you'll need to put some muscle behind it.

After drilling the holes, sand them so there are no rough edges.

- Finish the towel rack with a stain of your choice.

Wall-Mounted Coat Rack

There is a lot of room for creative expression with this one! Choose any kind of hook you have lying around or find in a store, placing as many or few as you like along the rack. For a more classic look, you may want to hold back on sanding after painting and use more ornate hooks.

Materials used:

Reciprocating or jigsaw
Sander with 60 grit paper
Electric Drill
5 used/vintage metal hooks
10 - #6 x ⅝″ screws
Acrylic paint
Spray paint
Stain

Instructions:

- Measure the desired size according to how many hooks you are planning to use.

- Select your desired hooks.

- Position the hooks on the pallet to plan out spacing and screw into place. Alternatively, you can pre-drill the holes.

▸ Remove the hardware and paint the rack.

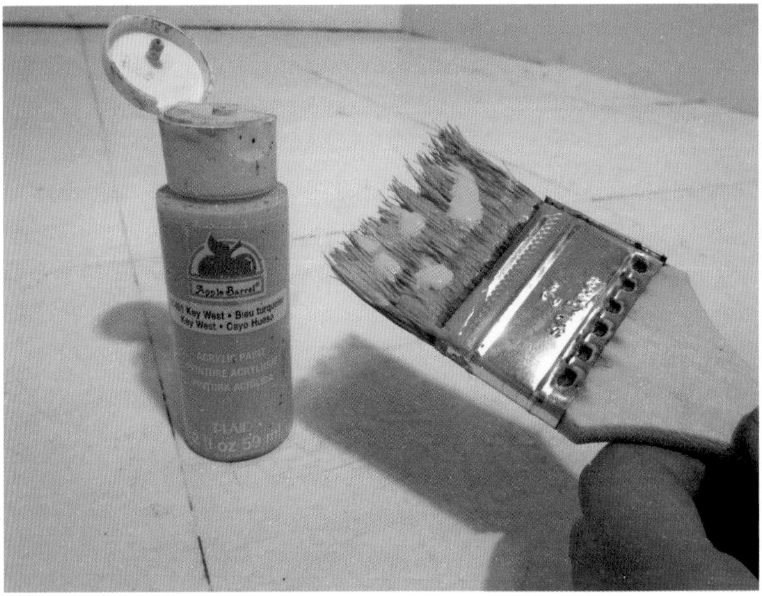

▸ Try using multiple shades of color at times to make the finish more interesting!

- Notice the slight variations even though it is mostly the featured color you picked out.

- For a distressed look, lightly sand off some of the paint.

Apply the stain with polyurethane in it for shine.

Wipe the surface with a clean cloth, removing excess stain for a weathered look.

▸ Notice the two boards on the right and the difference when stain is added.

▸ Spray paint your hooks black, or another color of your choosing. Allow the wood to dry and screw them back into place. Using a small paintbrush, finish the screws with acrylic paint for a shinier finish.

▸ Done and done! Hang the pallet using L–brackets that will stay hidden.

Sconces

These sconces are so easy to make and would fit in almost any room and design scheme. I kept mine pretty simple, but there is much room for added detail. You can stencil behind the candle or use mod podge to transfer an image to the back-board. Just make sure to place the candle at a space and height far enough to keep the flame away from the image.

Materials used:

Small nails
Wood Glue
Stain
Miter Saw
Reciprocating or jigsaw
Sander with 60 grit paper

Instructions:

- Use a small pallet with wide boards to allow for a variety of candle sizes. This may seem daunting, but it's actually so easy to cut angled pieces with a miter saw. Simply swing the guide from 0 degrees all the way to the right to 45 degrees and cut.

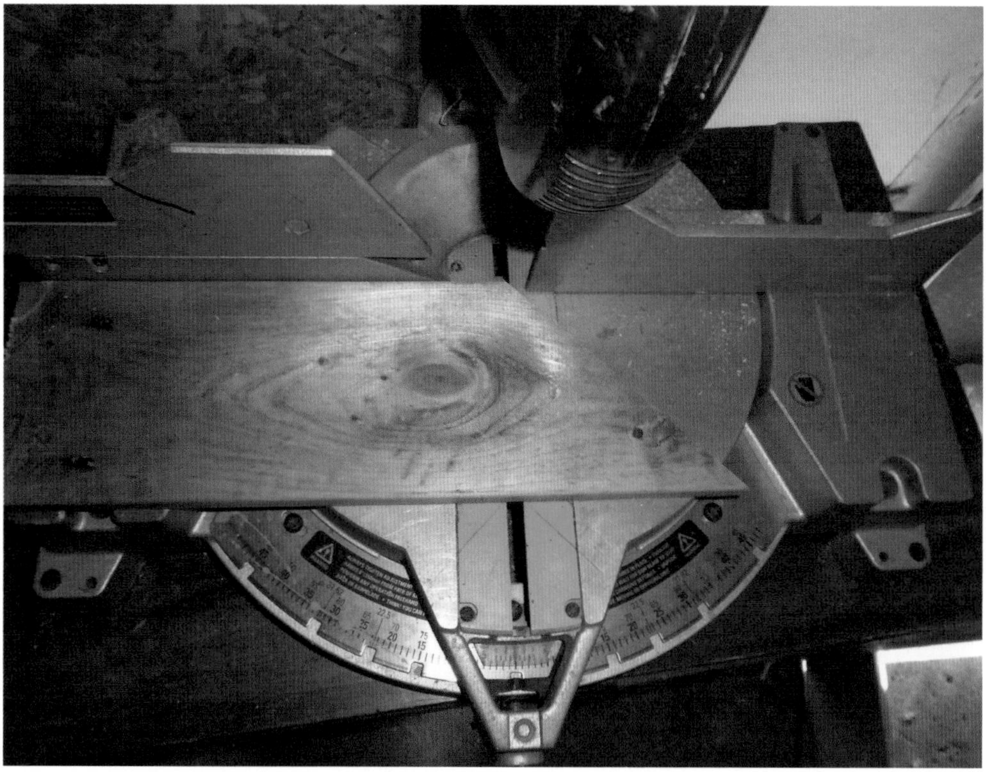

- Bring the blade back to the original spot at 0 degrees. Slide the board backwards so that the top of your angled cut is in the middle of the blade and make a straight cut down.

- Set the triangle piece aside and make one more angled cut on the leftover piece of the board.

- The result will be a matching triangle piece to make a set!

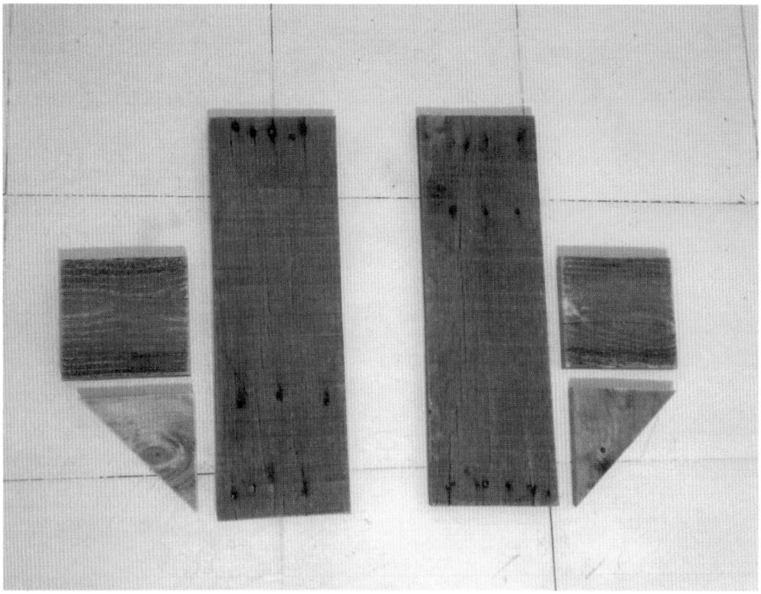

- You now have all your pieces to assemble two sconces.

- Glue your triangle piece first so you can best determine where to place the candle shelf.

Wipe off extra glue.

Glue on the candle shelf.

- Allow the glue to dry for at least thirty minutes.

- Hammer in some small nails for extra support.

▸ Hammer diagonally into tip of triangle piece.

▸ The stained gray offers a slight change, but not too different from the original look. The neutral background color is great for using candles of any color.

Just add candles!

Door Handle Serving Tray

This is the most popular item I have ever made. Although they are intended as serving trays, a lot of people use them purely as a display on coffee tables or kitchen counters, and some hang them on the wall as art. Using the type of handle that you can screw into from the top saves so much time and work. The only downside is that there is a much smaller variety of these types of handles as opposed to the kind you screw in from underneath the wood.

Materials used:

2 - ¼″ black hammer pulls
8 - #6 x ¾″ multipurpose screws
Reciprocating or jigsaw
Miter Saw
Electric drill
Sander with 60 grit paper
Spray paint
Polyurethane

Instructions:

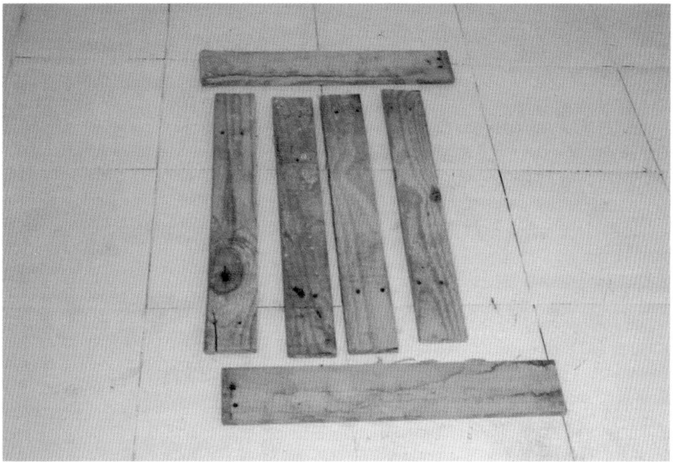

- Using three pallet boards, cut six pieces for the tray: four base boards and two for the handles. When making the trays, choose the best boards to make a flush, even tray. The individual boards often vary, so instead focus on the overall size of the tray you would like. However, the handle boards should match in size for aesthetic quality.

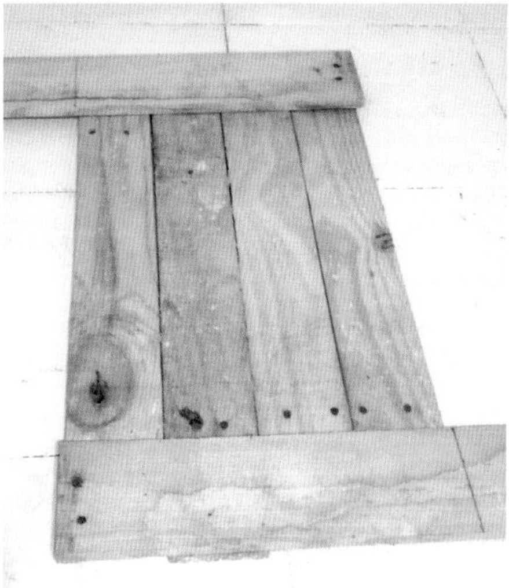

- Push the boards together before assembling. This is helpful to get measurements before you make your cuts.

- Make cuts with the miter saw and sand each piece. Flip the tray over and screw the baseboards into the bottoms of the handle boards. Make sure you screw deep enough that the screws don't stick out and scratch the surface of anything the tray may be placed on.

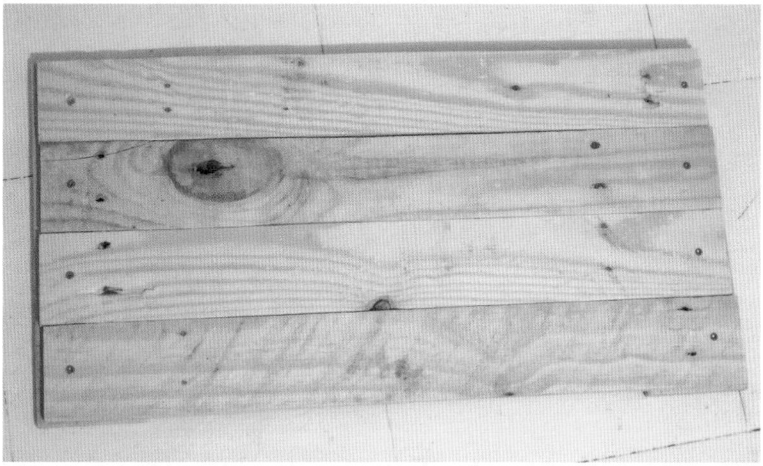

- One screw on each end of baseboard is usually enough, but use more if needed.

- Flip the tray right side up to examine for uneven pieces and to make sure the boards are screwed in straight.

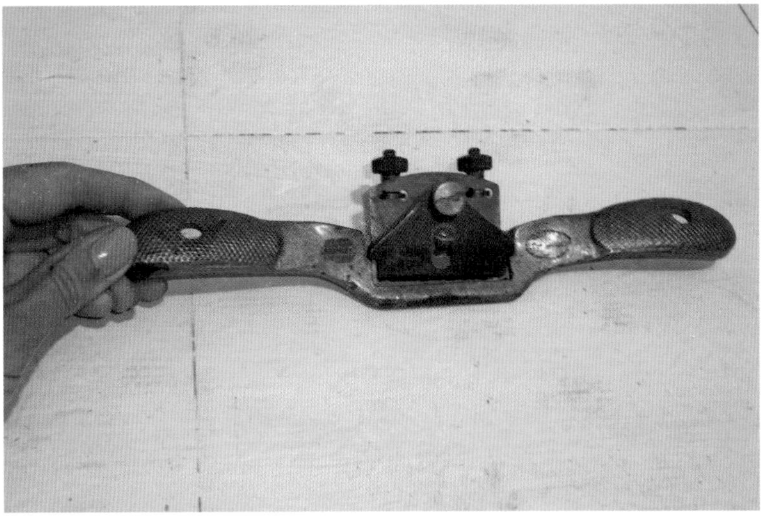

- If you have any pieces that have rough edges and may cause a problem when setting glasses on the tray, you may be able to fix the problem by sanding it or possibly using a hand plane. These babies are awesome and come in quite handy!

- I recommend using pulls that you can screw into from the top of the pull. There are a variety of handles out there you could use, but most have to be screwed in from the bottom of your board, as they are mostly used for cabinetry. I use these because trying to align those types of handles is a lot more work.

- For this part, you want to be exact. Otherwise, you may end up grabbing the handles unevenly and possibly spilling the contents of the tray onto the unsuspecting guests you are serving!

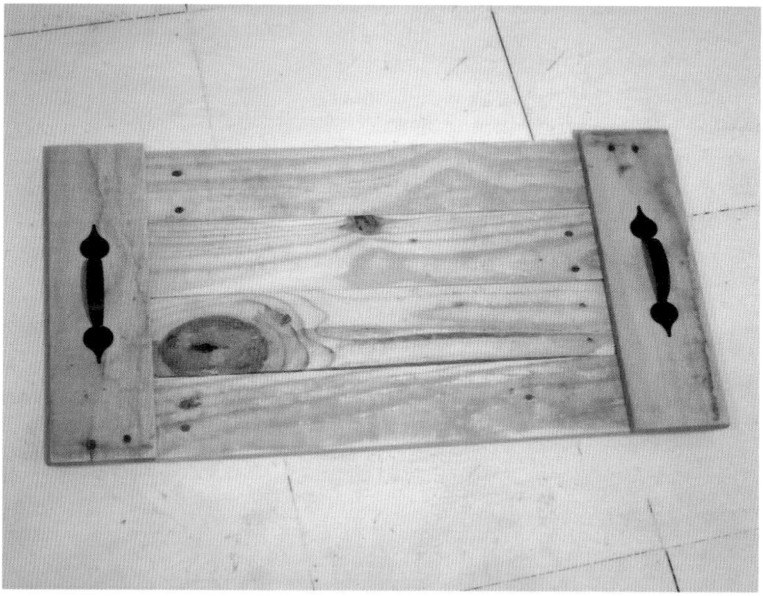

- Measure and drill the holes into the boards. You can come back and screw the pulls into place once the tray is painted.

- Lightly spray paint the tray in ivory. The light color allows you to see the wood and old nails still embedded in original pallet. Finish with polyurethane.

Wine Rack

This is a small-sized wine rack, but you can make them as wide as the pallet you use. Displaying your wine this way is inexpensive, attractive, and out of the way if you are hard-pressed for counter space. Cutting the holes in the bottom piece for hanging the glasses can be a learning process, but once you get a good one done, it may be helpful to save it as a guide for making glass holder boards in the future.

Materials used:

10 - #6 x 1¼″ multipurpose screws
Reciprocating or jigsaw
Miter saw
Sander with 60 grit paper
Electric drill
¾″ spade drill bit
Dremel tool

Instructions:

- Choose a pallet that has the basic shape of the rack.

- Using a reciprocating or jigsaw, cut the rack out of one corner of your pallet, making sure to include the outside and middle stringer boards so that the deck boards remain attached to them both. You will also need a board to wedge inside for the bottles to sit on and a bottom board that will hold the glasses.

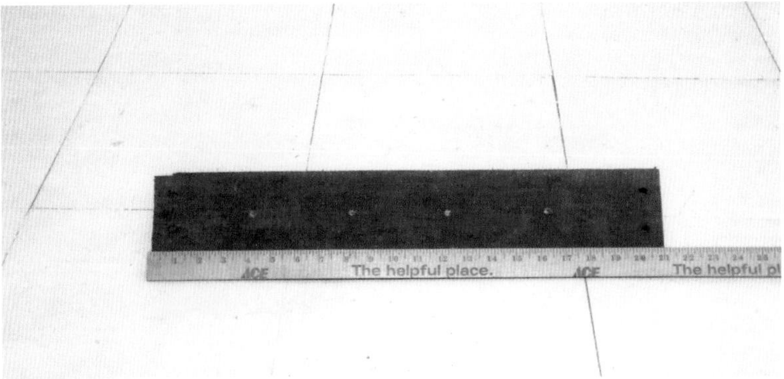

- Measure out spots to drill holes for your wine glasses to hang from. In this example, the board is 21 inches long and you are going to make four holes for glasses. Divide 21 by 4 and you have 5.25. This will be the spacing for your marks, 5¼″ apart.

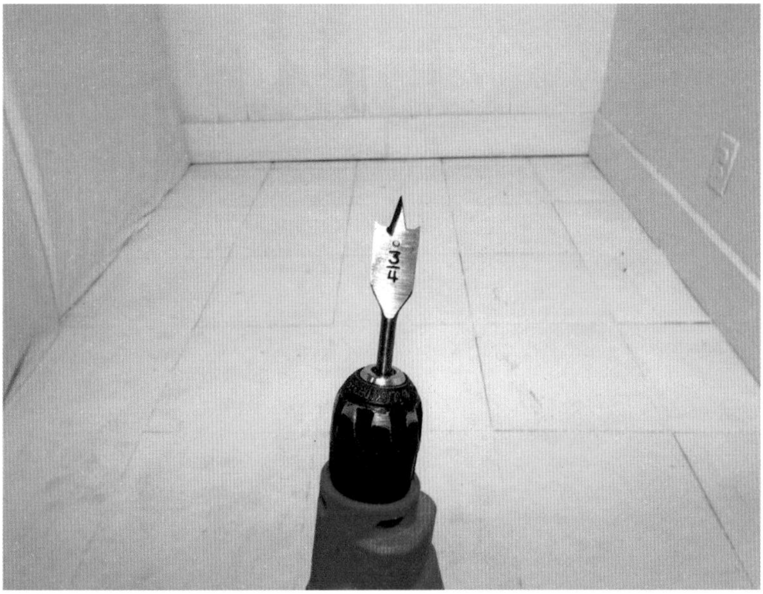

- Use a ¾″ spade drill bit to drill out holes. You will have to put some muscle behind it and make sure you hold the drill straight against the board.

- Yours holes should look fairly clean like the ones pictured, but if not, you can always go over them with a Dremel rotary tool. If you do not have one, sometimes you can get the job done with a jigsaw if you have a steady hand. Using a ruler, draw lines in pencil for your saw to follow to cut out remaining wood.

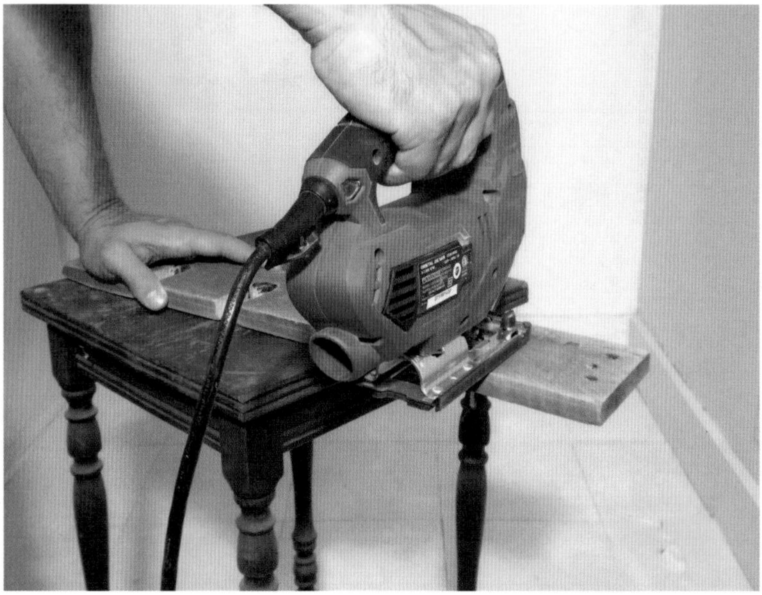

- Cut out the wood using a jigsaw. You can also use a reciprocating saw by clamping the board to a workbench or a table to hold it securely.

- The end result should look something like this!

- There are a couple of ways to get this middle board inside the wine rack. If it seems like the board is a close, tight fit, you can simply hammer it into place without taking the front board off. In this case, the front board was too long, blocking the glasses from sliding in and out with ease. It must be either shortened by trimming some of the wood off of the bottom while the board is still attached, or taken off and moved up a tiny amount. Since this board had room to be moved up, I went with the third option. While the front board is removed, place your board that sits inside in place.

- Screw the front board back on, leaving enough space at the bottom for glasses to slide in, while also pinching the inside board and holding it secure. If you want extra support for the inside board, drill one hole on each side of the rack where the board sits. Follow it with one 1¼″ screw in each side.

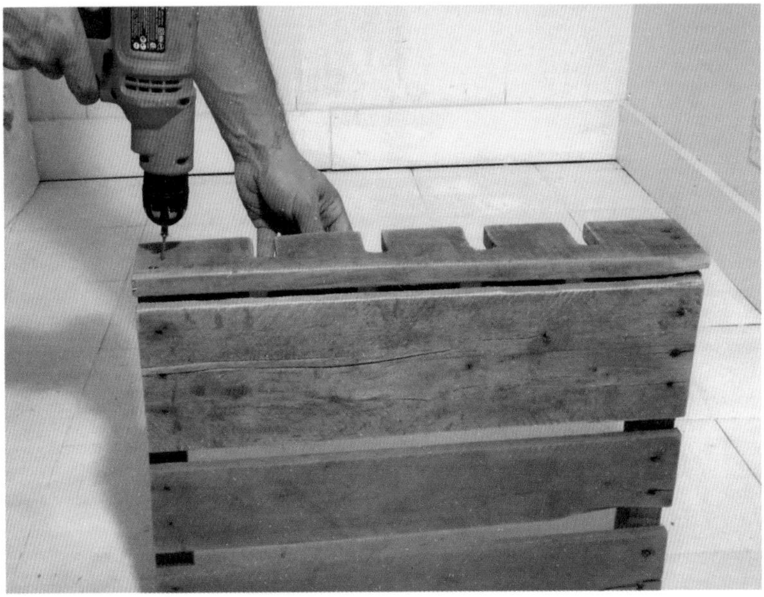

- Flip the wine rack upside down and secure the bottom piece with four 1¼″ screws, two on each end.

- I left this piece looking rustic, only coating it with polyurethane.

PART THREE

DÉCOR

Pallet Arrow Wall Art

These arrows are fun to use in decorating your wall, as a nameplate for a child's bedroom, or to use outdoors to point guests in the right direction. They take about ten minutes to make and you only need one or two deck boards.

Materials used:

Reciprocating or jigsaw
Miter saw
Wood glue
Sander with 60 grit paper

Instructions:

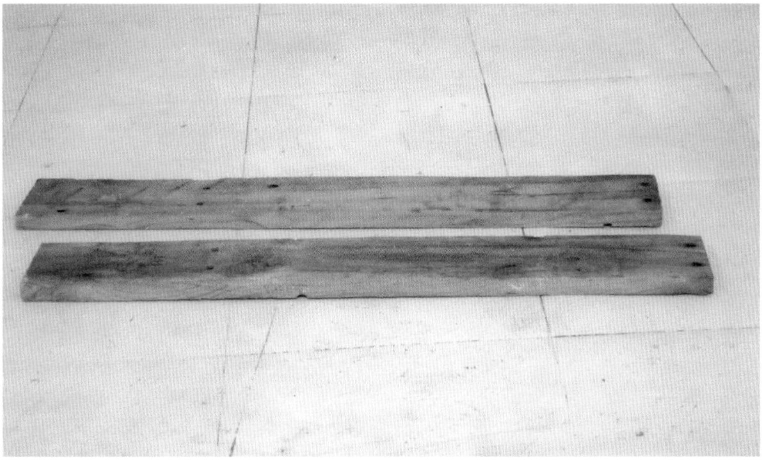

- Use either one long board or two medium-sized boards depending on the size of arrow you want.

Place board on miter saw, "good" side up, and cut off the end at a 30-degree angle.

Flip your board over. Starting at the point of your previous cut, make another 30-degree cut.

- This is the tip of your arrowhead.

- Flip your board over to the "good" side again. Place the tip piece as a guide to where you will make your next cut, and then mark with a pencil.

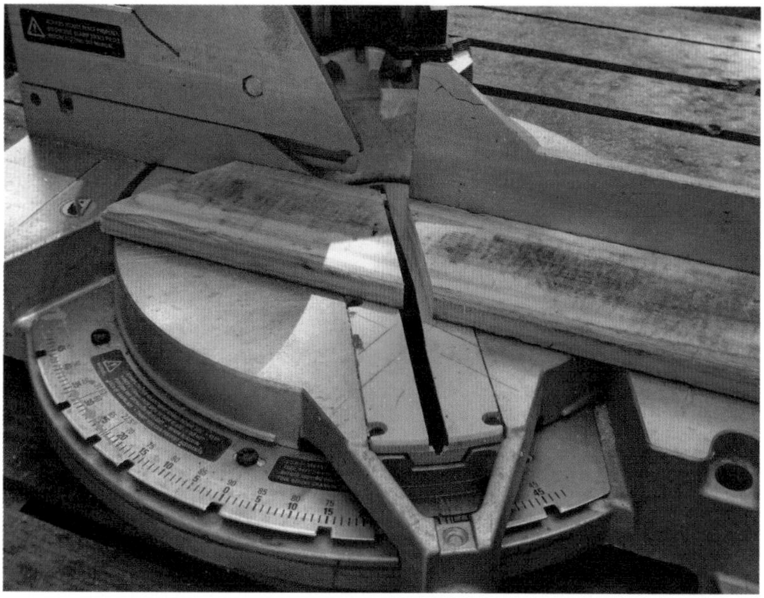

- Cut along the mark with a 30-degree angle.

- You have finished the arrowhead.

- Turn your board around so you are dealing with the uncut end of the "good" side and cut off the end at a 45-degree angle.

- Slide the board down to the desired length of the arrow feather and make another 45-degree cut.

- Flip the board over and use the already cut arrow feather as a guide for the last feather piece. Cut the wood at a 45-degree angle.

- You have finished the arrow feathers.

- If you would like to add more detail, line up feathers even and make two more 45-degree cuts.

- You now have all the pieces you need to assemble the arrow.

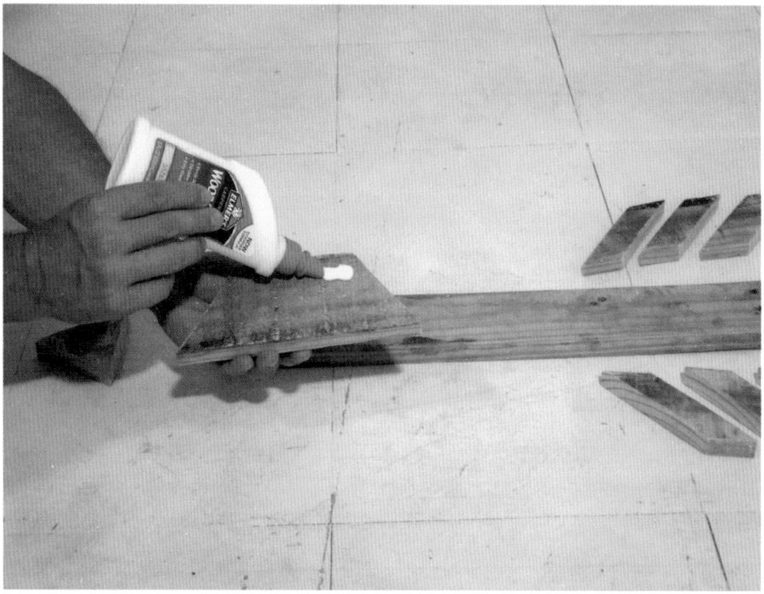

▸ Glue the pieces on and allow the piece to dry for 30 minutes.

▸ There are many ways to decorate these arrows, so have fun with it!

— Painted Wall Art —

If you search for pallet art on the Internet, you find a wide array of subjects and skill. Some crafters have specialized machines that help in making all those letters beautiful and straight, others are just that good at free hand. I have no machines and am not that good. I do have a printer though, and there is much you can do with just that! This project was so simple and worked on the first try, which is a rare experience for me with art projects!

Materials used:

Wood glue
Reciprocating or jigsaw
Miter saw
Sander with 60 grit paper
Spray paint
Cardstock
Spray adhesive
Acrylic paint
Stain

Instructions:

- Use even, smooth boards, ideally from the same pallet that are light in color.

- Make cuts to the desired size, along with two support boards. Sand the wood smooth.

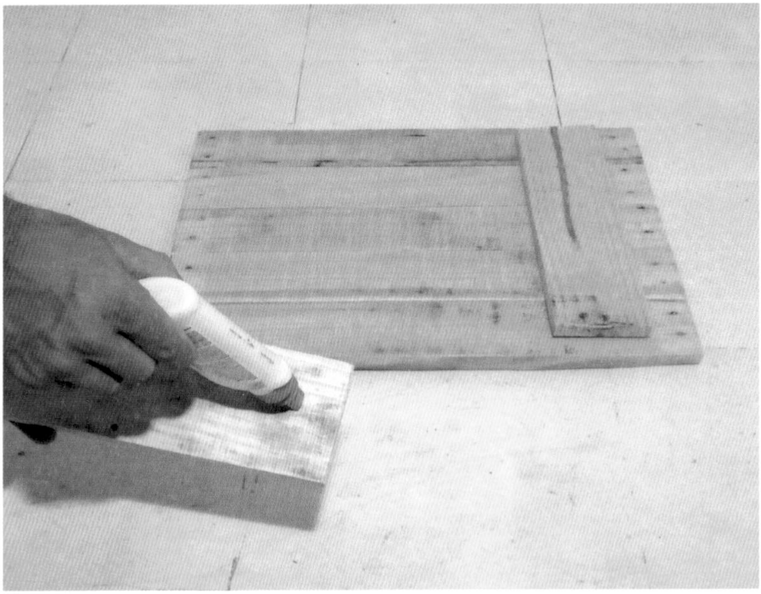

- Glue the support boards on the backside of the boards so they stay hidden.

- Allow the glue to dry for thirty minutes.

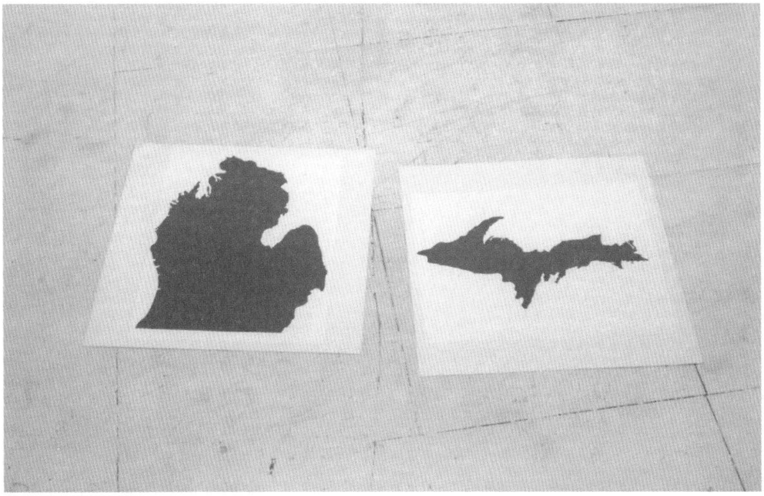

- Print any image you like. There are many sites on the Internet that offer free printables. Make sure you download one large enough for the size project you have in mind. Silhouette prints work well for making your own stencil. Once printed, stick it onto a piece of cardstock paper with spray adhesive so you will have a sturdier stencil.

- Cut out your stencil and arrange it to your liking on your pallet canvas. If you are having trouble keeping small pieces down on the boards, roll a small piece of Scotch tape and put it under the stencil to hold it in place.

- Using a can of spray paint, lay the board flat on the ground and completely cover the stencil and the board. Make sure you spray it with medium coverage; spraying on too much might cause drips that could seep under the stencil edges.

- Wait for the paint to dry enough so that it will not smear, about ten minutes or so, and then remove the stencil.

- Since this project is of my home state, I cut out a heart to place over the city I live in. Trace the heart and paint it any color.

This project was much easier than expected, and I will definitely be doing more of this in the future. I sanded the heart to distress lightly and sealed the entire piece with a polyshade.

Outdoor Flower Box

This flower box is basically a large pallet shelf, only not as tall. It is important to note how you assemble the bottom board so you can hold in dirt, but also still allow water to drain. If necessary, you can always drill tiny holes into the bottom board for water flow. Sealing this piece with polyurethane is a must if you want it to last.

Materials used:

4 - #6 x 1¼″ multipurpose screws
$^{3}/_{32}$″ drill bit
Reciprocating or jigsaw
Electric drill
Sander with 60 grit paper
Stain

Instructions:

- Use a pallet that is long enough for the window where it will be hung.

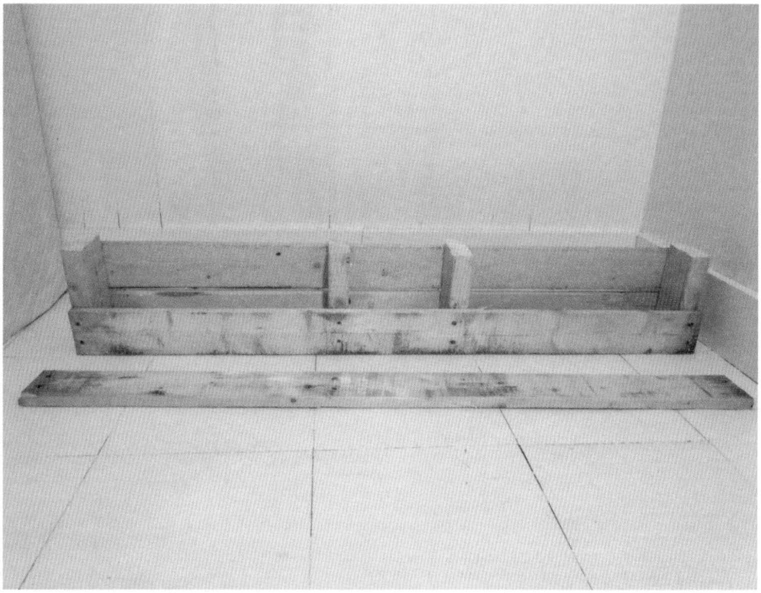

- Cut off one end of pallet with the saw and an extra board to use as the bottom of the box.

- Sand the pieces. Flip the box upside down and align the bottom piece to drill holes for screws.

- Drill in four 1¼″ screws so that there is one for each stringer board. The bottom board should fit on nice and tight, but with enough space for water to get through when watering plants. If you find that there is too much space between boards, you can use a plastic plant liner that will fit into the box unseen, or use wire screen to shape inside and hold the dirt in place.

- Finished with a polyshade, which is stain plus polyurethane.

- There is no standard for how to attach pallets to the outside of your home, though this flower box is attached to the underside of the window using L-brackets. You can also consider screwing it into the back board of the flower box, straight into the siding. Just do whatever works for you!

Flower Arrangement Centerpiece

These boxes can be used in so many ways! They are great for tables at weddings and parties but can also be useful as decorative mail holders or charger boxes for your devices. In this case, you can drill holes into the back board to allow cords to hang out and not get tangled. I use mine by the front door to throw keys and cell phones in so they are where I need them when I am ready to head out.

Materials used:

4 - 1½ x ⅝″ corner iron brackets
14 - #6 x ⅝″ screws
Wood glue
Miter Saw
Reciprocating or jigsaw
Sander with 60 grit paper
Electric Drill
Clamps
Acrylic paint
Stain
4 mason jars

Instructions:

- Using a couple of pallet boards, cut five pieces for the box.

- Make cuts using a miter saw or whatever you have available that will cut straight.

- Sand the pieces and arrange them so that the boards will support each other when you start gluing.

- Start with a short end piece by applying wood glue to the sides and bottom of the board.

▸ Continue gluing the remaining boards.

▸ Clamp and allow the piece to dry for at least thirty minutes.

- Once dried, screw in the L-brackets using $\frac{5}{8}''$ screws on each corner for extra support.

- Paint the piece in your desired colors. Fill the mason jars with water and flowers and place inside for a lovely display!

Clothespin Picture Frame

The tricky part with making a pallet picture frame is always the glass. This frame is very simple to make, requires no glass, and is more accessible for switching out old pictures and updating your wall. You could use a variety of different clips to hang your photos or stencil designs on the edges of your frame.

Materials used:

Wood clothespins
Wood glue
Reciprocating or jigsaw
Miter saw
Acrylic paint

Instructions:

- Cut the boards for the size of frame you would like, as well as two extra to hold it together.
- Sand the wood smooth.

- Place the boards next to each other and glue the support pieces on perpendicularly, either on front if you would like them to show, or hidden on the back.

- Allow the glue to dry for thirty minutes.

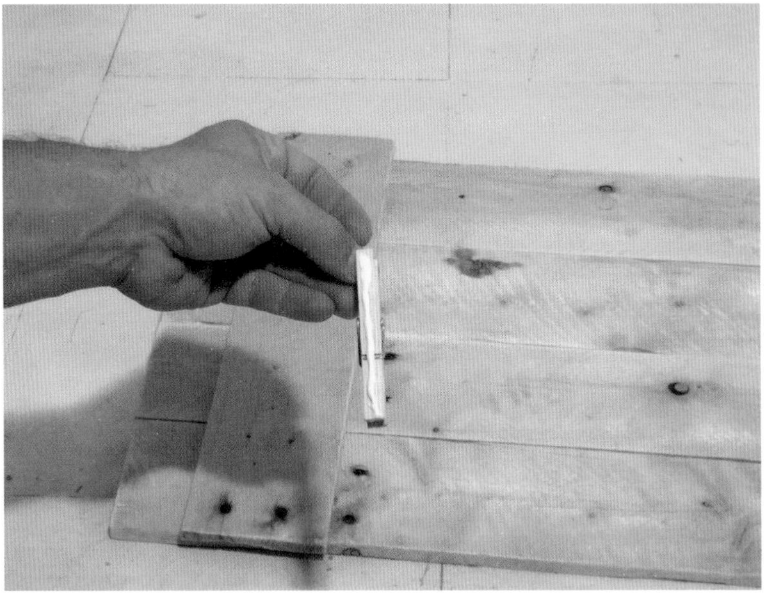

▸ Glue on the wooden clothespins at the desired height. Allow the glue to dry for thirty minutes before painting.

▸ This frame has a "sketched" look to it that I achieved by painting it yellow and then brushing black over the cracks, edges, and clothespins with a tiny paintbrush.

AUTHOR BIO

Danny Darke is an amateur photographer and small business owner. She built Skid Row Palletes literally from the ground up, starting in her basement two years ago. When she isn't covered in stain, she is playing cards with her husband, Chris, and daughter, Frankie. Born and raised in the Metro-Detroit area where she still resides, she credits the spirit of Detroit for her hardworking attitude: "If you want something done, Do It Yourself!" You can visit her at skidrowpalletes.com.